*Occult Symbolism of Animals,
Insects, Reptiles,
Fish and Birds*

By Manly P. Hall

Copyright © 2019 Lamp of Trismegistus. All rights reserved. No part of this publication may be reproduced or transmitted in any form or by any means, electronic or mechanical, including photocopying, recording, or by any information storage and retrieval system, without permission in writing from Lamp of Trismegistus. Reviewers may quote brief passages.

ISBN: 978-1-63118-420-8

Esoteric Classics

Other Books in this Series and Related Titles

The Devil in Love by Jacques Cazotte (978–1–63118–499–4)

A Weird Tale & Other Supernatural Stories by W Q Judge (978–1–63118–518–2)

Magical Essays and Instructions by Florence Farr (978-1-63118-418-5)

On the Cave of the Nymphs in the Odyssey by Thomas Taylor (978-1-63118-505-2)

Rosicrucian Rules, Secret Signs, Codes and Symbols by various (978–1–63118–488–8)

The Janeites, The Man Who Would Be King and Other Stories of Freemasonry by Rudyard Kipling (978–1–63118–480–2)

The Treasure of Atlantis by J Allan Dunn (978-1-63118-522-9)

The Poem of Hashish by A Crowley & C Baudelaire (978-1-63118-484-0)

The Great God Pan by Arthur Machen (978–1–63118–528–1)

The Star and the Garter by Aleister Crowley (978-1-63118-406-2)

Hermetic Arcanum by Jean d'Espagnet (978-1-63118-519-9)

Thirty–One Hymns to the Star Goddess by Frater Achad (978–1–63118–422–2)

A Collection of Magical Writings, Fiction, Poetry & Essays by Aleister Crowley (978–63118–424–6)

With the Adepts or An Adventure Among the Rosicrucians (978-1-63118-523-6)

The Sword of Welleran and Other Stories by Lord Dunsany (978-1-63118-501-4)

The Smoky God or A Voyage to the Inner World by Emerson (978-1-63118-423-9)

The Inmost Light and Other Tales by Arthur Machen (978–1–63118–531–1)

A Collection of Fiction and Essays by Occult Writers on Supernatural and Metaphysical Subjects by various (978–1–63118–510–6)

The A. E. Waite Reader: A Selection of Occult Essays (978–1–63118–515–1)

The Leadbeater Reader: A Selection of Occult Essays (978–1–63118–483–3)

Audio versions are also available on Audible, Amazon and Apple

Other Books in this Series and Related Titles

Paracelsus, the Four Elements and Their Spirits by M P Hall (978-1-63118-400-0)

The Magician's Heavenly Chaos by Thomas Vaughan (978-1-63118-500-7)

Masonic and Rosicrucian History by M P Hall & H Voorhis (978-1-63118-486-4)

Tao Te Ching & Commentary by Lao Tzu & C Johnston (978-1-63118-495-6)

The Influence of Pythagoras on Freemasonry and Other Essays (978-1-63118-404-8)

The Golden Verses of Pythagoras: Five Translations (978-1-63118-479-6)

On the Philadelphian Gold by Philochrysus & Philadelphus (978-1-63118-511-3)

The Secret Book of the Philosopher's Stone by Artephius (978-1-63118-517-5)

Aurora of the Philosophers by Paracelsus (978-1-63118-507-6)

A Collection of Early Writings on Astral Travel (978-1-63118-477-2)

The First and Second Gospels of the Infancy of Jesus Christ (978-1-63118-415-4)

The Old Past Master by Carl H Claudy (978-1-63118-464-2)

The Path of Light: A Manual of Maha-Yana Buddhism (978-1-63118-471-0)

The Hymns of Hermes by G. R. S. Mead (978-1-63118-405-5)

Clairvoyance and Psychic Abilities by Leadbeater & Besant (978-1-63118-403-1)

The Human Aura: Astral Colors and Thought Forms (978-1-63118-419-2)

The Feminine Occult by various authors (978-1-63118-711-7)

Ancient Mysteries and Secret Societies by M P Hall (978-1-63118-410-9)

A Collection of Writings Related to Occult, Esoteric, Rosicrucian and Hermetic Literature, Including Freemasonry, the Kabbalah, the Tarot, Alchemy and Theosophy
various authors *Volumes 1-4*
(978-1-63118-713-1) (978-1-63118-714-8)
(978-1-63118-715-5) (978-1-63118-716-2)

Audio Versions are also available on Audible, Amazon and Apple

Table of Contents

Introduction…7

Part I: Prologue…9

Part II: Fish…11

Part III: Insects…17

Part IV: Reptiles…27

Part V: Composite Creatures…33

Part VI: Birds…35

Part VII: The Phoenix…41

Part VIII: Animals…47

INTRODUCTION

The word "esoteric" can be difficult to define. Esotericism in general can be seen less as a system of beliefs and more as a category, which encompasses numerous, different systems of beliefs. It's a bit of juxtaposition, since the word "esoteric" indicates something that few people know about, while the term itself broadly covers numerous philosophies, practices, areas of study and belief systems.

In a greater sense, Esotericism acts as a storehouse for secret knowledge, which is often considered ancient (by *tradition, if not by fact),* passed down from generation to generation, in private. At various times in history, simply possessing the knowledge of some of these subjects, was considered illegal and a jailable offence, if discovered. This usually included such general topics as Alchemy, Pharmacology, Qabalah, Hermeticism, Occultism, Ceremonial Magic, Astrology, Divination, Rosicrucianism and so on. Collectively, these areas of study were often referred to as the esoteric sciences.

Sometimes, the outer garment of a subject isn't esoteric, while what is hidden beneath it, is. As an example, Freemasonry isn't necessarily esoteric by nature (at *least not anymore),* but certain signs, passwords and handshakes given to the candidate during their initiation, are in fact, esoteric, in the sense that they are hidden from the general public.

Today, in the twenty-first century, such topics are readily available at bookstores across the country, and numerous mainsteam publishers offer beginners guides and coffee-table volumes on many of these subjects, intended for mass appeal. Books like *"The Secret"* have turned previously arcane topics into household knowledge. All that being the case, however, it isn't to say that there still aren't buried secrets to uncover, ancient wisdom being ignored and forgotten mysteries to be explored. In fact, it is often that we are only able to further our own studies by standing on the shoulders of these disappearing giants.

Lamp of Trismegistus is doing its part to help preserve humanity's esoteric history by making some of these classics available to those students who are seeking to unearth the knowledge of these ancient colossi.

So, be sure to check other titles from our *Esoteric Classics* series, as well as our *Occult Fiction*, *Theosophical Classics*, *Foundations of Freemasonry Series*, *Supernatural Fiction*, *Paranormal Research Series*, *Studies in Buddhism* and our *Christian Apocrypha Series*. You can also download the audio versions of most of these titles from Amazon, Apple or Audible, for learning on the go.

Part I:
Prologue

The creatures inhabiting the water, air, and earth were held in veneration by all races of antiquity. Realizing that visible bodies are only symbols of invisible forces, the ancients worshiped the Divine Power through the lower kingdoms of Nature, because those less evolved and more simply constituted creatures responded most readily to the creative impulses of the gods. The sages of old studied living things to a point of realization that God is most perfectly understood through a knowledge of His supreme handiwork--animate and inanimate Nature.

Every existing creature manifests some aspect of the intelligence or power of the Eternal One, who can never be known save through a study and appreciation of His numbered but inconceivable parts. When a creature is chosen, therefore, to symbolize to the concrete human mind some concealed abstract principle it is because its characteristics demonstrate this invisible principle in visible action. Fishes, insects, animals, reptiles, and birds appear in the religious symbolism of nearly all nations, because the forms and habits of these creatures and the media in which they exist closely relate them to the various generative and germinative powers of Nature, which were considered as prima- facie evidence of divine omnipresence.

Primitive peoples believed the sea and land were inhabited by strange creatures, and early books on zoology contain curious illustrations of composite beasts, reptiles, and fishes, which did not exist at the time the mediæval authors compiled these voluminous books. In the ancient initiatory rituals of the Persian, Greek, and Egyptian Mysteries the priests disguised themselves as composite creatures, thereby symbolizing different aspects of human consciousness. They used birds and reptiles as emblems of their various deities, often creating forms of grotesque appearance and assigning to them imaginary traits, habits, and places of domicile, all of which were symbolic of certain spiritual and transcendental truths thus concealed from the profane. The *phoenix* made its nest of incense and flames. The *unicorn* had the body of a horse, the feet of an elephant, and the tail of a wild boar. The upper half of the *centaur's* body was human and the lower half equine. The *pelican* of the Hermetists fed its young from its own breast, and to this bird were assigned other mysterious attributes which could have been true only allegorically.

Though regarded by many writers of the Middle Ages as actual living creatures, none of these--the pelican excepted--ever existed outside the symbolism of the Mysteries. Possibly they originated in rumors of animals then little known. In the temple, however, they became a reality, for there they signified the manifold characteristics of man's nature. The *mantichora* had certain points in common with the hyena; the *unicorn* may have been the single-horned rhinoceros. To the student of the secret wisdom these composite animals. and birds simply represent various forces working in the invisible worlds. This is a point which nearly all writers on the subject of mediaeval monsters seem to have overlooked.

Part II:

Fish

The early philosophers and scientists, realizing that all life has its origin in water, chose the fish as the symbol of the life germ. The fact that fishes are most prolific makes the simile still more apt. While the early priests may not have possessed the instruments necessary to analyze the spermatozoon, they concluded by deduction that it resembled a fish.

Fishes were sacred to the Greeks and Romans, being connected with the worship of Aphrodite (Venus). An interesting survival of pagan ritualism is found in the custom of eating fish on Friday. *Freya,* in whose honor the day was named, was the Scandinavian Venus, and this day was sacred among many nations to the goddess of beauty and fecundity. This analogy further links the fish with the procreative mystery. Friday is also sacred to the followers of the Prophet Mohammed.

The Hebrew letter *nun* means both fish and growth, and as Inman says: "The Jews were led to victory by the Son of the Fish whose other names were Joshua and Jesus (the Savior). *Nun* is still the name of a female devotee" of the Christian faith. Among early Christians three fishes were used to symbolize the Trinity, and the fish is also one of the eight sacred symbols of the great Buddha. It is also significant that the dolphin should be sacred to both Apollo (the Solar Savior) and Neptune. It was believed that this fish carried shipwrecked sailors to heaven on its back. The dolphin was accepted by the early Christians as an emblem of Christ, because the pagans had viewed this beautiful creature as a friend and benefactor of man. The heir to the throne of France, *the Dauphin,* may have secured his title from this ancient pagan symbol of the divine preservative power. The first advocates of Christianity likened converts to fishes, who at the time of baptism "returned again into the sea of Christ."

There are also legends to the effect that long before the appearance of human beings there existed a race or species of composite creatures which was destroyed by the gods. The temples of antiquity preserved their own historical records and possessed information concerning the prehistoric world that has never been revealed to the uninitiated. According to these records, the human race evolved from a species of creature that partook somewhat of the nature of an amphibian, for at that time primitive man had the gills of a fish and was partly covered with scales. To a limited degree, the human embryo demonstrates the possibility of such a condition. As a result of the theory of man's origin in water, the fish was looked upon as the progenitor of the human family. This gave rise to the ichthyolatry of the Chaldeans, Phoenicians, and Brahmins. The American Indians believe that the waters of lakes, rivers, and oceans are inhabited by a mysterious people, the "Water Indians."

The fish has been used as an emblem of damnation; but among the Chinese it typified contentment and good fortune, and fishes appear on many of their coins. When Typhon, or Set, the Egyptian evil genius, had divided the body of the god

Osiris into fourteen parts, he cast one part into the river Nile, where, according to Plutarch, it was devoured by three fishes-- the *lepidotus* (probably the *lepidosiren*), the *phagrus,* and the *oxyrynchus* (a form of pike). For this reason the Egyptians would not eat the flesh of these fishes, believing that to do so would be to devour the body of their god. When used as a symbol of evil, the fish represented the earth (man's lower nature) and the tomb (the sepulcher of the Mysteries). Thus was Jonah three days in the belly of the great fish," as Christ was three days in the tomb.

Several early church fathers believed that the "whale" which swallowed Jonah was the symbol of God the Father, who, when the hapless prophet was thrown overboard, accepted Jonah into His own nature until a place of safety was reached. The story of Jonah is really a legend of initiation into the Mysteries, and the "great fish" represents the darkness of ignorance which engulfs man when he is thrown over the side of the ship (is born) into the sea (life). The custom of building ships in the form of fishes or birds, common in ancient times, could give rise to the story, and mayhap Jonah was merely picked up by another vessel and carried into port, the pattern of the ship causing it to be called a "great fish." ("*Veritatis simplex oratio est!*") More probably the "whale" of Jonah is based upon the pagan mythological creature, *hippocampus,* part horse and part dolphin, for the early Christian statues and carvings show the composite creature and not a true whale.

It is reasonable to suppose that the mysterious sea serpents, which, according to the Mayan and Toltec legends, brought the gods to Mexico were Viking or Chaldean ships, built in the shape of composite sea monsters or dragons. H. P. Blavatsky advances the theory that the word *cetus,* the great whale, is derived from *keto,* a name for the fish god, Dagon, and that Jonah was actually confined in a cell hollowed out in the body of a gigantic statue of Dagon after he had been captured by Phoenician sailors and carried to one of their cities. There is no doubt a great mystery in the gigantic form of *cetus,* which is still preserved as a constellation.

According to many scattered fragments extant, man's lower nature was symbolized by a tremendous, awkward creature resembling a great sea serpent, or dragon, called *leviathan.* All symbols having serpentine form or motion signify the solar energy in one of its many forms. This great creature of the sea therefore represents the solar life force imprisoned in water and also the divine energy coursing through the body of man, where, until transmuted, it manifests itself as a writhing, twisting monster--- man's greeds, passions, and lusts. Among the symbols of Christ as the Savior of men are a number relating to the mystery of His divine nature concealed within the personality of the lowly Jesus.

The Gnostics divided the nature of the Christian Redeemer into two parts--the one Jesus, a mortal man; the other, Christos, a personification of *Nous,* the principle of Cosmic Mind. *Nous,* the greater, was for the period of three years (from baptism to crucifixion) using the fleshly garment of the mortal man (Jesus). In order to illustrate this point and still conceal it from the ignorant, many strange, and often repulsive, creatures were used whose rough exteriors concealed magnificent organisms. Kenealy, in his notes on the *Book of Enoch,* observes: "Why the caterpillar was a symbol of the Messiah is evident; because, under a lowly, creeping, and wholly terrestrial aspect, he conceals the beautiful butterfly- form, with its radiant wings, emulating in its varied colors the Rainbow, the Serpent, the Salmon, the Scarab, the Peacock, and the dying Dolphin..."

Part III:

Insects

In 1609 Henry Khunrath's *Amphitheatrum Sapientiæ Æternæ* was published. Eliphas Levi declared that within its pages are concealed all the great secrets of magical philosophy. A remarkable plate in this work shows the Hermetic sciences being attacked by the bigoted and ignorant pedagogues of the seventeenth century. In order to express his complete contempt for his slanderers, Khunrath made out of each a composite beast, adding donkey ears to one and a false tail to another. He reserved the upper part of the picture for certain petty backbiters whom he gave appropriate forms. The air was filled with strange creatures--great dragon flies, winged frogs, birds with human heads, and other weird forms which defy description--heaping venom, gossip, spite, slander, and other forms of persecution upon the secret arcanum of the wise. The drawing indicated that their attacks were ineffectual. Poisonous insects were often used to symbolize the deadly power of the human tongue.

Insects of all kinds were also considered emblematic of the Nature spirits and demons, for both were believed to inhabit the atmosphere. Mediaeval drawings showing magicians in the act of invoking spirits, often portray the mysterious powers of the other world, which the conjurer has exorcised, as appearing to him in composite part-insect forms. The early philosophers apparently held the opinion that the disease which swept through communities in the form of plagues were actually living creatures, but instead of considering a number of tiny germs they viewed the entire plague as one individuality and gave it a hideous shape to symbolize its destructiveness. The fact that plagues came in the air caused an insect or a bird to be used as their symbol.

Beautiful symmetrical forms were assigned to all-natural benevolent conditions or powers, but to unnatural or malevolent powers were assigned contorted and abnormal figures. The Evil One was either hideously deformed or else of the nature of certain despised animals. A popular superstition during the Middle Ages held that the Devil had the feet of a rooster, while the Egyptians assigned to Typhon (the Devil) the body of a hog.

The habits of the insects were carefully studied. Therefore the ant was looked upon as emblematic of industry and foresight, as it stored up supplies for the winter and also had strength to move objects many times its own weight. The locusts which swept down in clouds, and in some parts of Africa and Asia obscured the sun and destroyed every green thing, were considered fit emblems of passion, disease, hate, and strife; for these emotions destroy all that is good in the soul of man and leave a barren desert behind them. In the folklore of various nations, certain insects are given special significance, but the ones which have received world-wide veneration and consideration ate the scarab, the king of the insect kingdom; the scorpion, the great betrayer; the butterfly, the emblem of metamorphosis; and the bee, the symbol of industry.

The Egyptian scarab is one of the most remarkable symbolic figures ever conceived by the mind of man. It was evolved by the erudition of the priestcraft from a simple insect which, because of its peculiar habits and appearance, properly symbolized the strength of the body, the resurrection of the soul, and the Eternal and Incomprehensible Creator in His aspect as Lord of the Sun. E. A. Wallis Budge says, in effect, of the worship of the scarab by the Egyptians:

> *"Yet another view held in primitive times was that the sky was a vast meadow over which a huge beetle crawled, pushing the disk of the sun before him. This beetle was the Sky-god, and, arguing from the example of the beetle, which was observed to roll along with its hind legs a ball that was believed to contain its eggs, the early Egyptians thought that the ball of the Sky- god contained his egg and that the sun was his offspring. Thanks, however, to the investigations of the eminent entomologist, Monsieur J. H. Fabre, we now know that the ball which the beetle rolls along contains not its eggs, but dung that is to serve as food for its egg, which it lays in a carefully prepared place."*

Initiates of the Egyptian Mysteries were sometimes called scarabs; again, lions and panthers. The scarab was the emissary of the sun, symbolizing light, truth, and regeneration. Stone scarabs, called heart scarabs, about three inches long, were placed in the heart cavity of the dead when that organ was removed to be embalmed separately as part of the process of mummifying. Some maintain that the stone beetles were merely wrapped in the winding cloths at the time of preparing the body for eternal preservation. The following passage concerning this appears in the great Egyptian book of initiation, *The Book of the*

Dead: "And behold, thou shalt make a scarab of green stone, which shalt be placed in the breast of a man, and it shall perform for him, 'the opening of the mouth.'" The funeral rites of many nations bear a striking resemblance to the initiatory ceremonies of their Mysteries.

Ra, the god of the sun, had three important aspects. As the Creator of the universe he was symbolized by the head of a scarab and was called *Khepera,* which signified the resurrection of the soul and a new life at the end of the mortal span. The mummy cases of the Egyptian dead were nearly always ornamented with scarabs. Usually one of these beetles, with outspread wings, was painted on the mummy case directly over the breast of the dead. The finding of such great numbers of small stone scarabs indicates that they were a favorite article of adornment among the Egyptians. Because of its relationship to the sun, the scarab symbolized the divine part of man's nature. The fact that its beautiful wings were concealed under its glossy shell typified the winged soul of man hidden within its earthly sheath. The Egyptian soldiers were given the scarab as their special symbol because the ancients believed that these creatures were all of the male sex and consequently appropriate emblems of virility, strength, and courage.

Plutarch noted the fact that the scarab rolled its peculiar ball of dung backwards, while the insect itself faced the opposite direction. This made it an especially fitting symbol for the sun, because this orb (according to Egyptian astronomy) was rolling from west to east, although apparently moving in the opposite direction. An Egyptian allegory states that the sunrise is caused by the scarab unfolding its wings, which stretch out as glorious colors on each side of its body--the solar globe--and that when it folds its wings under its dark shell at sunset, night follows. *Khepera,* the scarab-headed aspect of *Ra,* is often symbolized riding through the sea of the sky in a wonderful ship called the *Boat of the Sun.*

The scorpion is the symbol of both wisdom and self-destruction. It was called by the Egyptians the creature accursed; the time of year when the sun entered the sign of Scorpio marked the beginning of the rulership of Typhon. When the twelve signs of the zodiac were used to represent the twelve Apostles (although the reverse is *actually* true), the scorpion was assigned to Judas Iscariot--the betrayer.

The scorpion stings with its tail, and for this reason it has been called a backbiter, a false and deceitful thing. Calmet, in his *Dictionary of the Bible,* declares the scorpion to be a fit emblem of the wicked and the symbol of persecution. The dry winds of Egypt are said to be produced by Typhon, who imparts to the sand the blistering heat of the infernal world and the sting of the scorpion. This insect was also the symbol of the spinal fire which, according to the Egyptian Mysteries, destroyed man when it was permitted to gather at the base of his spine (the tail of the scorpion). The red star *Antares* in the back of the celestial scorpion was considered the worst light in the heavens. *Kalb al Akrab,* or the heart of the scorpion, was called by the ancients the lieutenant or deputy of Mars. *Antares* was believed to impair the eyesight, often causing blindness if it rose over the horizon when a child was born. This may refer again to the sand storm, which was capable of blinding unwary travelers.

The scorpion was also the symbol of wisdom, for the fire which it controlled was capable of illuminating as well as consuming. Initiation into the Greater Mysteries among the pagans was said to take place only in the sign of the scorpion. In the papyrus of *Ani* (The *Book of the Dead*), the deceased likens his soul to a scorpion, saying: "I am a swallow, I am that scorpion, the daughter of Ra!" Elizabeth Goldsmith, in her treatise on *Sex Symbolism,* states that the scorpions were a "symbol of Selk, the Egyptian goddess of writing, and also [were] revered by the

Babylonians and Assyrians as guardians of the gateway of the sun. Seven scorpions were said to have accompanied Isis when she searched for the remains of Osiris scattered by Set" (Typhon).

In his *Chaldean Account of the Genesis,* George Smith, copying from the cuneiform cylinders, in describing the wanderings of the hero *Izdubar* (Nimrod), throws some light on the scorpion god who guards the sun. The tablet which he translated is not perfect, but the meaning is fairly clear: "...who each day guard the rising sun. Their crown was at the lattice of heaven, under hell their feet were placed [the spinal column]. The scorpion man guarded the gate, burning with terribleness, their appearance was like death, the might of his fear shook the forest. At the rising of the sun and the setting of the sun, they guarded the sun; Izdubar saw them and fear and terror came into his face." Among the early Latins there was a machine of war called the scorpion. It was used for firing arrows and probably obtained its name from a long beam, resembling a scorpion's tail, which flew up to hurl the arrows. The missiles discharged by this machine were also called scorpions.

The butterfly (under the name of *Psyche,* a beautiful maiden with wings of opalescent light) symbolizes the human soul because of the stages it passes through in order to unfold its power of flight. The three divisions through which the butterfly passes in its unfoldment resemble closely the three degrees of the Mystery School, which degrees are regarded as consummating the unfoldment of man by giving him emblematic wings by which he may soar to the skies. Unregenerate man, ignorant and helpless, is symbolized by the stage between ovum and larva; the disciple, seeking truth and dwelling in medication, by the second stage, from larva to pupa, at which time the insect enters its chrysalis (the tomb of the Mysteries); the third stage, from pupa to imago (wherein the perfect butterfly comes forth), typifies the unfolded enlightened soul of the initiate rising from the tomb of his baser nature.

Night moths typify the secret wisdom, because they are hard to discover and are concealed by the darkness (ignorance). Some are emblems of death, such as *Acherontia atropos,* the death's-head moth, which has a marking on its body somewhat like a human skull. The death-watch beetle, which was believed to give warning of approaching death by a peculiar ticking sound, is another instance of insects involved in human affairs.

Opinions differ concerning the spider. Its shape makes it an appropriate emblem of the nerve plexus and ganglia of the human body. Some Europeans consider it extremely bad luck to kill a spider-- possibly because it is looked upon as an emissary of the Evil One, whom no person desires to offend. There is a mystery concerning all poisonous creatures, especially insects. Paracelsus taught that the spider was the medium for a powerful but evil force which the Black Magicians used in their nefarious undertakings.

Certain plants, minerals, and animals have been sacred among all the nations of the earth because of their peculiar sensitiveness to the astral fire--a mysterious agency in Nature which the scientific world has contacted through its manifestations as electricity and magnetism. Lodestone and radium in the mineral world and various parasitic growths in the plant kingdom are strangely susceptible to this cosmic electric fire, or universal life force. The magicians of the Middle Ages surrounded themselves with such creatures as bats, spiders, cats, snakes, and monkeys, because they were able to appropriate the life forces of these species and use them to the attainment of their own ends. Some ancient schools of wisdom taught that all poisonous insects and reptiles are germinated out of the evil nature of man, and that when intelligent human beings no longer breed hate in their own souls there will be no more ferocious animals, loathsome diseases, or poisonous plants and insects.

Among the American Indians is the legend of a "Spider Man," whose web connected the heaven worlds with the earth. The secret schools of India symbolize certain of the gods who labored with the universe during its making as connecting the realms of light with those of darkness by means of webs. Therefore the builders of the cosmic system who held the embryonic universe together with threads of invisible force were sometimes referred to as the Spider Gods and their ruler was designated The Great Spider.

The beehive is found in Masonry as a reminder that in diligence and labor for a common good true happiness and prosperity are found. The bee is a symbol of wisdom, for as this tiny insect collects pollen from the flowers, so men may extract wisdom from the experiences of daily life. The bee is sacred to the goddess Venus and, according to mystics, it is one of several forms of life which came to the earth from the planet Venus millions of years ago. Wheat and bananas are said to be of similar origin. This is the reason why the origin of these three forms of life cannot be traced. The fact that bees are ruled by queens is one reason why this insect is considered a sacred feminine symbol.

In India the god Prana--the personification of the universal life force--is sometimes shown surrounded by a circle of bees. Because of its importance in pollinizing flowers, the bee is the accepted symbol of the generative power. At one time the bee was the emblem of the French kings. The rulers of France wore robes embroidered with bees, and the canopies of their thrones were decorated with gigantic figures of these insects.

The fly symbolizes the tormentor, because of the annoyance it causes to animals. The Chaldean god Baal was often called Baal-Zebul, or the god of the dwelling place. The word *zebub,* or *zabab,* means a fly, and Baal-Zebul became Baalzebub, or Beelzebub, a word which was loosely translated to mean Jupiter's fly. The fly was looked upon as a form of the divine power, because of its ability to destroy decaying substances and thus promote health. The fly may have obtained its name Zebub from its peculiar buzzing or humming. Inman believes that Baalzebub, which the Jews ridiculed as My Lord of Flies, really means My Lord Who Hums or Murmurs.

Inman recalls the singing Memnon on the Egyptian desert, a tremendous figure with an Aeolian harp on the top of its head. When the wind blows strongly this great Statue sings, or hums. The Jews changed Baalzebub into Beelzebub, and made him their prince of devils by interpreting *dæmon* as "demon." Naudaeus, in defending Virgil from accusations of sorcery, attempted a wholesale denial of the miracles supposedly performed by Virgil and produced enough evidence to convict the poet on all counts. Among other strange fears, Virgil fashioned a fly out of brass, and after certain mysterious ceremonies, placed it over one of the gates of Naples. As a result, no flies entered the city for more than eight years.

Part IV:

Reptiles

The serpent was chosen as the head of the reptilian family. Serpent worship in some form has permeated nearly all parts of the earth. The serpent mounds of the American Indian; the carved-stone snakes of Central and South America; the hooded cobras of India; Python, the great snake of the Greeks; the sacred serpents of the Druids; the Midgard snake of Scandinavia; the Nagas of Burma, Siam, and Cambodia; the brazen serpent of the Jews; the mystic serpent of Orpheus; the snakes at the Oracle of Delphi twining themselves around the tripod upon which the Pythian priestess sat, the tripod itself being in the form of twisted serpents; the sacred serpents preserved in the Egyptian temples; the Uraeus coiled upon the foreheads of the Pharaohs and priests;--all these bear witness to the universal veneration in which the snake was held. In the ancient Mysteries the serpent entwining a staff was the symbol of the physician. The serpent-wound staff of Hermes remains the emblem of the medical profession. Among nearly all these ancient peoples the serpent was accepted as the symbol of wisdom or salvation. The antipathy which Christendom feels towards the snake is based upon the little-understood allegory of the Garden of Eden.

The serpent is true to the principle of wisdom, for it tempts man to the knowledge of himself. Therefore the knowledge of self, resulted from man's disobedience to the *Demiurgus,* Jehovah. How the serpent came to be in the garden of the Lord after God had declared that all creatures which He had made during the six days of creation were good has not been satisfactorily answered by the interpreters of Scripture. The tree that grows in the midst of the garden is the spinal fire; the knowledge of the use of that spinal fire is the gift of the great serpent. Notwithstanding statements to the contrary, the serpent is the symbol and prototype of the Universal Savior, who redeems the worlds by giving creation the knowledge of itself and the realization of good and evil. If this be not so, why did Moses raise a brazen serpent upon a cross in the wilderness that all who looked upon it might be saved from the sting of the lesser snakes? Was not the brazen serpent a prophecy of the crucified Man to come? If the serpent be only a thing of evil, why did Christ instruct His disciples to be as wise as serpents?

The accepted theory that the serpent is evil cannot be substantiated. It has long been viewed as the emblem of immortality. It is the symbol of reincarnation, or metempsychosis, because it annually sheds its skin, reappearing, as it were, in a new body. There is an ancient superstition to the effect that snakes never die except by violence and that, if uninjured, they would live forever. It was also believed that snakes swallowed themselves, and this resulted in their being considered emblematic of the Supreme Creator, who periodically reabsorbed His universe back into Himself.

In *Isis Unveiled,* H. P. Blavatsky makes this significant statement concerning the origin of serpent worship: "Before our globe had become egg-shaped or round it was a long trail of cosmic dust or fire-mist, moving and writhing like a serpent. This, say the explanations, was the Spirit of God moving on the chaos until its breath had incubated cosmic matter and made it assume the annular shape of a serpent with its tail in its mouth--emblem of eternity in its spiritual and of our world in its physical sense."

The seven-headed snake represents the Supreme Deity manifesting through His Elohim, or Seven Spirits, by whose aid He established His universe. The coils of the snake have been used by the pagans to symbolize the motion and also the orbits of the celestial bodies, and it is probable that the symbol of the serpent twisted around the egg--which was common to many of the ancient Mystery schools-- represented both the apparent motion of the sun around the earth, and the bands of astral light, or the great magical agent, which move about the planet incessantly.

Electricity was commonly symbolized by the serpent because of its motion. Electricity passing between the poles of a spark gap is serpentine in its motion. Force projected through atmosphere was called The Great Snake. Being symbolic of universal force, the serpent was emblematic of both good and evil. Force can tear down as rapidly as it can build up. The serpent with its tail in its mouth is the symbol of eternity, for in this position the body of the reptile has neither beginning nor end. The head and tail represent the positive and negative poles of the cosmic life circuit. The initiates of the Mysteries were often referred to as serpents, and their wisdom was considered analogous to the divinely inspired power of the snake. There is no doubt that the title "Winged Serpents" (*the Seraphim*) was given to one of the invisible hierarchies that labored with the earth during its early formation.

There is a legend that in the beginning of the world winged serpents reigned upon the earth. These were probably the demigods which antedate the historical civilization of every nation. The symbolic relationship between the sun and the serpent found literal witness in the fact that life remains in the snake until sunset, even though it be cut into a dozen parts. The Hopi Indians consider the serpent to be in close communication with the Earth Spirit. Therefore, at the time of their annual snake dance they send their prayers to the Earth Spirit by first specially sanctifying large numbers of these reptiles and then liberating them to return to the earth with the prayers of the tribe.

The great rapidity of motion manifested by lizards has caused them to be associated with Mercury, the Messenger of the Gods, whose winged feet traveled infinite distances almost instantaneously. A point which must not be overlooked in connection with reptiles in symbolism is clearly brought out by the eminent scholar, Dr. H. E. Santee, in his *Anatomy of the Brain and Spinal Cord:* "In reptiles there are two pineal bodies, an anterior and a posterior, of which the posterior remains undeveloped but the anterior forms a rudimentary, cyclopean eye. In the Hatteria, a New Zealand lizard, it projects through the parietal foramen and presents an imperfect lens and retina and, in its long stalk, nerve fibers."

Crocodiles were regarded by the Egyptians both as symbols of Typhon and emblems of the Supreme Deity, of the latter because while under water the crocodile is capable of seeing--Plutarch asserts-- though its eyes are covered by a thin membrane. The Egyptians declared that no matter how far away the crocodile laid its eggs, the Nile would reach up to them in its next inundation, this reptile being endowed with a mysterious sense capable of making known the extent of the flood months before it took place. There were two kinds of crocodiles. The larger and more ferocious was hated by the Egyptians, for they likened it to the nature of Typhon, their destroying demon. Typhon waited to devour all who failed to pass the judgment of the Dead, which rite took place in the Hall of Justice between the earth and the Elysian Fields. Anthony Todd Thomson thus describes the good treatment accorded the smaller and tamer crocodiles, which the Egyptians accepted as personifications of good: "They were fed daily and occasionally had mulled wine poured down their throats. Their ears were ornamented with rings of gold and precious stones, and their forefeet adorned with bracelets."

To the Chinese the turtle was a symbol of longevity. At a temple in Singapore a number of sacred turtles are kept, their age recorded by carvings on their shells. The American Indians use the ridge down the back of the turtle shell as a symbol of the Great Divide between life and death. The turtle is a symbol of wisdom because it retires into itself and is its own protection. It is also a phallic symbol, as its relation to long life would signify. The Hindus symbolized the universe as being supported on the backs of four great elephants who, in turn, are standing upon an immense turtle which is crawling continually through chaos.

Part V:

Composite Creatures

The Egyptian sphinx, the Greek centaur, and the Assyrian man-bull have much in common. All are composite creatures combining human and animal members; in the Mysteries all signify the composite nature of man and subtly refer to the hierarchies of celestial beings that have charge of the destiny of mankind. These hierarchies are the *twelve holy animals* now known as constellations--star groups which are merely symbols of impersonal spiritual impulses. Chiron, the centaur, teaching the sons of men, symbolizes the intelligences of the constellation of Sagittarius, who were the custodians of the secret doctrine while (geocentrically) the sun was passing through the sign of Gemini. The five-footed Assyrian man-bull with the wings of an eagle and the head of a man is a reminder that the invisible nature of man has the wings of a god, the head of a man, and the body of a beast. The same concept was expressed through the sphinx--that armed guardian of the Mysteries who, crouching at the gate of the temple, denied entrance to the profane. Thus placed between man and his divine possibilities, the sphinx also represented the secret doctrine itself. Children's fairy stories abound with descriptions of symbolic monsters, for nearly all such tales are based upon the ancient mystic folklore.

Part VI:

Birds

As appropriate emblems of various human and divine attributes birds were included in religious and philosophic symbolism that of pagans and of Christians alike. Cruelty was signified by the buzzard; courage by the eagle; self-sacrifice by the pelican; and pride by the peacock. The ability of birds to leave the earth and fly aloft toward the source of light has resulted in their being associated with aspiration, purity, and beauty. Wings were therefore often added to various terrene creatures in an effort to suggest transcendency. Because their habitat was among the branches of the sacred trees in the hearts of ancient forests, birds were also regarded as the appointed messengers of the tree spirits and Nature gods dwelling in these consecrated groves, and through their clear notes the gods themselves were said to speak. Many myths have been fabricated to explain the brilliant plumage of birds. A familiar example is the story of Juno's peacock, in whose tail feathers were placed the eyes of Argus. Numerous American Indian legends also deal with birds and the origin of the various colors of feathers. The Navahos declare that when all living things climbed to the stalk of a bamboo to escape the Flood, the wild turkey was on the lowest branch and his tail feathers trailed in the water; hence the color was all washed out.

Gravitation, which is a law in the material world, is the impulse toward the center of materiality; levitation, which is a law in the spiritual world, is the impulse toward the center of spirituality. Seeming to be capable of neutralizing the effect of gravity, the bird was said to partake of a nature superior to other terrestrial creation; and its feathers, because of their sustaining power, came to be accepted as symbols of divinity, courage, and accomplishment. A notable example is the dignity attached to eagle feathers by the American Indians, among whom they are insignia of merit. Angels have been invested with wings because, like birds, they were considered to be the intermediaries between the gods and men and to inhabit the air or middle kingdom betwixt heaven and earth. As the dome of the heavens was likened to a skull in the Gothic Mysteries, so the birds which flew across the sky were regarded as thoughts of the Deity. For this reason Odin's two messenger ravens were called Hugin and Munin--*thought* and *memory*.

Among the Greeks and Romans, the eagle was the appointed bird of Jupiter and consequently signified the swiftly moving forces of the Demiurgus; hence it was looked upon as the mundane lord of the birds, in contradistinction to the phoenix, which was symbolic of the celestial ruler. The eagle typified the sun in its material phase and also the immutable Demiurgic law beneath which all mortal creatures must bend. The eagle was also the Hermetic symbol of sulphur, and signified the mysterious fire of Scorpio--the most profoundly significant sign of the zodiac and the *Gate of the Great Mystery*. Being one of the three symbols of Scorpio, the eagle, like the Goat of Mendes, was an emblem of the theurgic art and the secret processes by which the infernal fire of the scorpion was transmuted into the spiritual *light-fire* of the gods.

Among certain American Indian tribes the thunderbird is held in peculiar esteem. This divine creature is said to live above the clouds; the flapping of its wings causes the rumbling which accompanies storms, while the flashes from its eyes are the lightning. Birds were used to signify the vital breath; and among the Egyptians, mysterious hawklike birds with human heads, and carrying in their claws the symbols of immortality, are often shown hovering as emblems of the liberated soul over the mummified bodies of the dead. In Egypt the hawk was the sacred symbol of the sun; and Ra, Osiris, and Horus are often depicted with the heads of hawks. The cock, or rooster, was a symbol of Cashmala (or Cadmillus) in the Samothracian Mysteries, and is also a phallic symbol sacred to the sun. It was accepted by the Greeks as the emblem of Ares (Mars) and typified watchfulness and defense. When placed in the center of a weather vane it signifies the sun in the midst of the four corners of creation. The Greeks sacrificed a rooster to the gods at the time of entering the Eleusinian Mysteries. Sir Francis Bacon is supposed to have died as the result of stuffing a fowl with snow. May this not signify Bacon's initiation into the pagan Mysteries which still existed in his day?

Both the peacock and the ibis were objects of veneration because they destroyed the poisonous reptiles which were popularly regarded as the emissaries of the infernal gods. Because of the myriad of eyes in its tail feathers the peacock was accepted as the symbol of wisdom, and on account of its general appearance it was often confused with the fabled phoenix of the Mysteries. There is a curious belief that the flesh of the peacock will not putrefy even though kept for a considerable time. As an outgrowth of this belief the peacock became the emblem of immortality, because the spiritual nature of man--like the flesh of this bird--is incorruptible.

The Egyptians paid divine honors to the ibis and it was a cardinal crime to kill one, even by accident. It was asserted that the ibis could live only in Egypt and that if transported to a foreign country it would die of grief. The Egyptians declared this bird to be the preserver of crops and especially worthy of veneration because it drove out the winged serpents of Libya which the wind blew into Egypt. The ibis was sacred to Thoth, and when its head and neck were tucked under its wing its body closely resembled a human heart. The black and white ibis was sacred to the moon; but all forms were revered because they destroyed crocodile eggs, the crocodile being a symbol of the detested Typhon.

Nocturnal birds were appropriate symbols of both sorcery and the secret divine sciences: sorcery because black magic cannot function in the light of truth (day) and is powerful only when surrounded by ignorance (night); and the divine sciences because those possessing the arcana are able to see through the darkness of ignorance and materiality. Owls and bats were consequently often associated with either witchcraft or wisdom. The goose was an emblem of the first primitive substance or condition from which and within which the worlds were fashioned. In the Mysteries, the universe was likened to an egg which the Cosmic Goose had laid in space. Because of its blackness the crow was the symbol of chaos or the chaotic darkness preceding the light of creation. The grace and purity of the swan were emblematic of the spiritual grace and purity of the initiate. This bird also represented the Mysteries which unfolded these qualities in humanity. This explains the allegories of the gods (the secret wisdom) incarnating in the body of a swan (the initiate).

Being scavengers, the vulture, the buzzard, and the condor signified that form of divine power which by disposing of refuse and other matter dangerous to the life and health of humanity cleanses and purifies the lower spheres. These birds were therefore adopted as symbols of the disintegrative processes which accomplish good while apparently destroying, and by some religions have been mistakenly regarded as evil. Birds such as the parrot and raven were accorded veneration because, being able to mimic the human voice, they were looked upon as links between the human and animal kingdoms.

The dove, accepted by Christianity as the emblem of the Holy Ghost, is an extremely ancient and highly revered pagan yonic emblem. In many of the ancient Mysteries it represented the third person of the Creative Triad, or the Fabricator of the world. As the lower worlds were brought into existence through a generative process, so the dove has been associated with those deities identified with the procreative functions. It is sacred to Astarte, Cybele, Isis, Venus, Juno, Mylitta, and Aphrodite. On account of its gentleness and devotion to its young, the dove was looked upon as the embodiment of the maternal instinct. The dove is also an emblem of wisdom, for it represents the power and order by which the lower worlds are maintained. It has long been accepted as a messenger of the divine will, and signifies the activity of God.

The name dove has been given to oracles and to prophets. The true name of the dove was *Ionah* or *Ionas*; it was a very sacred emblem, and at one time almost universally received; it was adopted by the Hebrews; and the mystic Dove was regarded as a symbol from the days of Noah by all those who were of the Church of God. The prophet sent to Ninevah as God's messenger was called Jonah or the Dove; our Lord's forerunner, the Baptist, was called in Greek by the name of Ioannes; and so was the Apostle of Love, the author of the fourth Gospel and of the Apocalypse, named Ioannes.

In Masonry the dove is the symbol of purity and innocence. It is significant that in the pagan Mysteries the dove of Venus was crucified upon the four spokes of a great wheel, thus foreshadowing the mystery of the crucified Lord of Love. Although Mohammed drove the doves from the temple at Mecca, occasionally he is depicted with a dove sitting upon his shoulder as the symbol of divine inspiration. In ancient times the effigies of doves were placed upon the heads of scepters to signify that those bearing them were overshadowed by divine prerogative. In mediaeval art, the dove frequently was pictured as an emblem of divine benediction.

Part VII:

The Phoenix

Clement, one of the Ante-Nicene Fathers, describes, in the first century after Christ, the peculiar nature and habits of the phoenix, in this way:

> *"There is a certain bird which is called a Phoenix. This is the only one of its kind and lives five hundred years. And when the time of its dissolution draws near that it must die, it builds itself a nest of frankincense, and myrrh, and other spices, into which, when the time is fulfilled, it enters and dies. But as the flesh decays a certain kind of worm is produced, which, being nourished by the juices of the dead bird, brings forth feathers. Then, when it has acquired strength, it takes up that nest in which are the bones of its parent, and bearing these it passes from the land of Arabia into Egypt, to the city called Heliopolis. And, in open day, flying in the sight of all men, it places them on the altar of the sun, and having done this, hastens back to its former abode. The priests then inspect the registers of the dates, and find that it has returned exactly as the five hundredth year was completed."*

Although admitting that he had not seen the phoenix bird (there being only one alive at a time), Herodotus amplifies a bit the description given by Clement:

> *"They tell a story of what this bird does which does not seem to me to be credible: that he comes all the way from Arabia, and brings the parent bird, all plastered with myrrh, to the temple of the sun, and there buries the body. In order to bring him, they say, he first*

forms a ball of myrrh as big as he finds that he can carry; then he hollows out the ball, and puts his parent inside; after which he covers over the opening with fresh myrrh, and the ball is then of exactly the same weight as at first; so he brings it to Egypt, plastered over as I have said, and deposits it in the temple of the sun. Such is the story they tell of the doings of this bird."

Both Herodotus and Pliny noted the general resemblance in shape between the phoenix and the eagle, a point which the reader should carefully consider, for it is reasonably certain that the modern Masonic eagle was originally a phoenix. The body of the phoenix is described as having been covered with glossy purple feathers, while its long tail feathers were alternately blue and red. Its head was light in color and about its neck was a circlet of golden plumage. At the back of its head the phoenix had *a peculiar tuft of feathers*, a fact quite evident, although it has been overlooked by most writers and symbolists.

The phoenix was regarded as sacred to the sun, and the length of its life (500 to 1000 years) was taken as a standard for measuring the motion of the heavenly bodies and also the cycles of time used in the Mysteries to designate the periods of existence. The diet of the bird was unknown. Some writers declare that it subsisted upon the atmosphere; others that it ate at rare intervals but never in the presence of man. Modern Masons should realize the special Masonic significance of the phoenix, for the bird is described as using sprigs of acacia in the manufacture of its nest.

The phoenix (which is the mythological Persian *roc*) is also the name of a Southern constellation, and therefore it has both an astronomical and an astrological significance. In all probability, the phoenix was the swan of the Greeks, the eagle of the Romans, and the peacock of the Far East. To the ancient mystics the phoenix was a most appropriate symbol of the immortality of the human soul, for just as the phoenix was reborn out of its own dead self seven times seven, so again and again the spiritual nature of man rises triumphant from his dead physical body.

Mediaeval Hermetists regarded the phoenix as a symbol of the accomplishment of alchemical transmutation, a process equivalent to human regeneration. The name *phoenix* was also given to one of the secret alchemical formula. The familiar pelican of the Rose Croix degree, feeding its young from its own breast, is in reality a phoenix, a fact which can be confirmed by an examination of the head of the bird. The ungainly lower part of the pelican's beak is entirely missing, the head of the phoenix being far more like that of an eagle than of a pelican. In the Mysteries it was customary to refer to initiates as *phoenixes* or *men who had been born again*, for just as physical birth gives man consciousness in the physical world, so the neophyte, after nine degrees in the womb of the Mysteries, was born into a consciousness of the Spiritual world. This is the mystery of initiation to which Christ referred when he said, "Except a man be born again, he cannot see the kingdom of God" (John iii. 3). The phoenix is a fitting symbol of this spiritual truth.

European mysticism was not dead at the time the United States of America was founded. The hand of the Mysteries controlled in the establishment of the new government, for the signature of the Mysteries may still be seen on the Great Seal of the United States of America. Careful analysis of the seal discloses a mass of occult and Masonic symbols, chief among them the so-called American eagle--a bird which Benjamin Franklin declared unworthy to be chosen as the emblem of a great, powerful, and progressive people. Here again only the student of symbolism can see through the subterfuge and realize that the American eagle upon the Great Seal is but a conventionalized phoenix, a fact plainly discernible from an examination of the original seal. In his sketch of *The History of the Seal of the United States*,

Gaillard Hunt unwittingly brings forward much material to substantiate the belief that the original seal carried the Phoenix bird on its obverse surface and the Great Pyramid of Giza upon its reverse surface. In a colored sketch submitted as a design for the Great Seal by William Barton in 1782, an actual phoenix appears sitting upon a nest of flames. This itself demonstrates a tendency towards the use of this emblematic bird.

If any one doubts the presence of Masonic and occult influences at the time the Great Seal was designed, he should give due consideration to the comments of Professor Charles Eliot Norton of Harvard, who wrote concerning the unfinished pyramid and the All-Seeing Eye which adorned the reverse of the seal, as follows: "The device adopted by Congress is practically incapable of effective treatment; it can hardly (however artistically treated by the designer) look otherwise than as a dull emblem of a Masonic fraternity."

The eagles of Napoleon and Caesar and the zodiacal eagle of Scorpio are really phoenixes, for the latter bird--not the eagle--is the symbol of spiritual victory and achievement. Masonry will be in a position to solve many of the secrets of its esoteric doctrine when it realizes that both its single- and double-headed eagles are phoenixes, and that to all initiates and philosophers the phoenix is the symbol of the transmutation and regeneration of the creative energy--commonly called the accomplishment of the Great Work. The double-headed phoenix is the prototype of an androgynous man, for according to the secret teachings there will come a time when the human body will have two spinal cords, by means of which vibratory equilibrium will be maintained in the body.

Not only were many of the founders of the United States Government Masons, but they received aid from a secret and august body existing in Europe, which helped them to establish this country for a peculiar and particular purpose known only to the initiated few. The Great Seal is the signature of this exalted body--unseen and for the most part unknown--and the unfinished pyramid upon its reverse side is a trestleboard setting forth symbolically the task to the accomplishment of which the United States Government was dedicated from the day of its inception.

Part VIII:

Animals

The lion is the king of the animal family and, like the head of each kingdom, is sacred to the sun, whose rays are symbolized by the lion's shaggy mane. The allegories perpetuated by the Mysteries (such as the one to the effect that the lion opens the secret book) signify that the solar power opens the seed pods, releasing the spiritual life within. There was also a curious belief among the ancients that the lion sleeps with his eyes open, and for this reason the animal was chosen as a symbol of vigilance. The figure of a lion placed on either side of doors and gateways is an emblem of divine guardianship. King Solomon was often symbolized as a lion. For ages the feline family has been regarded with peculiar veneration. In several of the Mysteries--most notably the Egyptian--the priests wore the skins of lions, tigers, panthers, pumas, or leopards. Hercules and Samson (both solar symbols) slew the lion of the constellation of Leo and robed themselves in his skin, thus signifying that they represented the sun itself when at the summit of the celestial arch.

At Bubastis in Egypt was the temple of the famous goddess Bast, the cat deity of the Ptolemies. The Egyptians paid homage to the cat, especially when its fur was of three shades or its eyes of different colors. To the priests the cat was symbolic of the magnetic forces of Nature, and they surrounded themselves with these animals for the sake of the astral fire which emanated from their bodies. The cat was also a symbol of eternity, for when it sleeps it curls up into a ball with its head and tail touching. Among the Greeks and Latins the cat was sacred to the goddess Diana. The Buddhists of India invested the cat with special significance, but for a different reason. The cat was the only animal absent at the death of the great Buddha, because it had stopped on the way to chase a mouse. That the symbol of the lower astral forces should not be present at the liberation of the Buddha is significant.

Regarding the cat, Herodotus says: "Whenever a fire breaks out, cats are agitated with a kind of divine motion, which they that keep them observe, neglecting the fire: The cats, however, in spite of their care, break from them, leaping even over the heads of their keepers to throw themselves into the fire. The Egyptians then make great mourning for their death. If a cat dies a natural death in a house, all they of that house shave their eyebrows: If a dog, they shave the head and all the body. They used to embalm their dead cats, and carry them to Bubastis to be interred in a sacred house.

The most important of all symbolic animals was the Apis, or Egyptian bull of Memphis, which was regarded as the sacred vehicle for the transmigration of the soul of the god Osiris. It was declared that the Apis was conceived by a bolt of lightning, and the ceremony attendant upon its selection and consecration was one of the most impressive in Egyptian ritualism. The Apis had to be marked in a certain manner. Herodotus states that the bull must be black with a square white spot on his forehead, the form of an eagle (probably a vulture) on his back, a beetle upon (under) his tongue, and the hair of his tail lying two ways. Other writers declare that the sacred bull was marked with twenty-nine sacred symbols, his body was spotted, and upon his right side was a white mark in the form of a crescent. After its sanctification the Apis was kept in a stable adjacent to the temple and led in processionals through the streets of the city upon certain solemn occasions. It was a popular belief among the Egyptians that any child upon whom the bull breathed would become illustrious. After reaching a certain age (twenty-five years) the Apis was taken either to the river Nile or to a sacred fountain (authorities differ on this point) and drowned, amidst the lamentations of the populace. The mourning and wailing for his death continued until the new Apis was found, when it was declared that Osiris had reincarnated, whereupon rejoicing took the place of grief.

The worship of the bull was not confined to Egypt, but was prevalent in many nations of the ancient world. In India, Nandi--the sacred white bull of Siva--is still the object of much veneration; and both the Persians and the Jews accepted the bull as an important religious symbol. The Assyrians, Phoenicians, Chaldeans, and even the Greeks revered this animal, and Jupiter turned himself into a white bull to abduct Europa. The bull was a powerful phallic emblem signifying the paternal creative power of the Demiurgus. At his death he was frequently mummified and buried with the pomp and dignity of a god in a specially prepared sarcophagus. Excavations in the Serapeum at Memphis have uncovered the tombs of more than sixty of these sacred animals.

As the sign rising over the horizon at the vernal equinox constitutes the starry body for the annual incarnation of the sun, the bull not only was the celestial symbol of the Solar Man but, because the vernal equinox took place in the constellation of Taurus, was called the *breaker* or *opener* of the year. For this reason in astronomical symbolism the bull is often shown breaking the annular egg with his horns. The Apis further signifies that the God-Mind is incarnated in the body of a beast and therefore that the physical beast form is the sacred vehicle of divinity. Man's lower personality is the Apis in which Osiris incarnates. The result of the combination is the creation of Sor-Apis (Serapis)-the material soul as ruler of the irrational material body and involved therein. After a certain period (which is determined by the square of five, or twenty-five years), the body of the Apis is destroyed and the soul liberated by the water which drowns the material life. This was indicative of the washing away of the material nature by the baptismal waters of divine light and truth. The drowning of the Apis is the symbol of death; the resurrection of Osiris in the new bull is the symbol of eternal renovation. The white bull was also symbolically sacred as the appointed emblem of the initiates, signifying the spiritualized material bodies of both man and Nature.

When the vernal equinox no longer occurred in the sign of Taurus, the Sun God incarnated in the constellation of Aries and the ram then became the vehicle of the solar power. Thus the sun rising in the sign of the Celestial Lamb triumphs over the symbolic serpent of darkness. The lamb is a familiar emblem of purity because of its gentleness and the whiteness of its wool. In many of the pagan Mysteries it signified the Universal Savior, and in Christianity it is the favorite symbol of

Christ. Early church paintings show a lamb standing upon a little hill, and from its feet pour four streams of living water signifying the four Gospels. The blood of the lamb is the solar life pouring into the world through the sign of Aries.

The goat is both a phallic symbol and also an emblem of courage or aspiration because of its surefootedness and ability to scale the loftiest peaks. To the alchemists the goat's head was the symbol of sulphur. The practice among the ancient Jews of choosing a scapegoat upon which to heap the sins of mankind is merely an allegorical depiction of the Sun Man who is the scapegoat of the world and upon whom are cast the sins of the twelve houses (tribes) of the celestial universe. Truth is the Divine Lamb worshiped throughout pagandom and slain for the sins of the world, and since the dawn of time the Savior Gods of all religions have been personifications of this Truth. The Golden Fleece sought by Jason and his Argonauts is the Celestial Lamb--the spiritual and intellectual sun. The secret doctrine is also typified by the Golden Fleece--the wool of the Divine Life, the rays of the Sun of Truth. Suidas declares the Golden Fleece to have been in reality a book, written upon skin, which contained the formulae for the production of gold by means of chemistry. The Mysteries were institutions erected for the transmutation of base ignorance into precious illumination. The dragon of ignorance was the terrible creature set to guard the Golden Fleece, and represents the darkness of the old year which battles with the sun at the time of its equinoctial passage.

Deer were sacred in the Bacchic Mysteries of the Greeks; the Bacchantes were often clothed in fawnskins. Deer were associated with the worship of the moon goddess and the

Bacchic orgies were usually conducted at night. The grace and speed of this animal caused it to be accepted as the proper symbol of esthetic abandon. Deer were objects of veneration with many nations. In Japan, herds of them are still maintained in connection with the temples.

The wolf is usually associated with the principle of evil, because of the mournful discordance of its howl and the viciousness of its nature. In Scandinavian mythology the Fenris Wolf was one of the sons of Loki, the infernal god of the fires. With the temple of Asgard in flames about them, the gods under the command of Odin fought their last great battle against the chaotic forces of evil. With frothing jowls the Fenris Wolf devoured Odin, the Father of the Gods, and thus destroyed the Odinic universe. Here the Fenris Wolf represents those mindless powers of Nature that overthrew the primitive creation.

The unicorn, or monoceros, was a most curious creation of the ancient initiates. It is described by Thomas Boreman as "a beast, which though doubted of by many writers, yet is by others thus described: He has but one horn, and that an exceedingly rich one, growing out of the middle of his forehead. His head resembles a hart's, his feet an elephant's, his tail a boar's, and the rest of his body a horse's. The horn is about a foot and half in length. His voice is like the lowing of an ox. His mane and hair are of a yellowish color. His horn is as hard as iron, and as rough as any file, twisted or curled, like a flaming sword; very straight, sharp, and every where black, excepting the point. Great virtues are attributed to it, in expelling of poison and curing of several diseases. He is not a beast of prey."

While the unicorn is mentioned several times in Scripture, no proof has yet been discovered of its existence. There are a number of drinking horns in various museums presumably fashioned from its spike. It is reasonably certain, however, that these drinking vessels were really made either from the tusks of some large mammal or the horn of a rhinoceros. J. P. Lundy believes that the horn of the unicorn symbolizes the hem of salvation mentioned by St. Luke which, pricking the hearts of men, turns them to a consideration of salvation through Christ. Mediaeval Christian mystics employed the unicorn as an emblem of Christ, and this creature must therefore signify the spiritual life in man. The single horn of the unicorn may represent the pineal gland, or third eye, which is the spiritual cognition center in the brain. The unicorn was adopted by the Mysteries as a symbol of the illumined spiritual nature of the initiate, the horn with which it defends itself being the flaming sword of the spiritual doctrine against, which nothing can prevail.

In the *Book of Lambspring,* a rare Hermetic tract, appears an engraving showing a deer and a unicorn standing together in a wood. The picture is accompanied by the following text: "The Sages say truly that two animals are in this forest: One glorious, beautiful, and swift, a great and strong deer; the other an unicorn... If we apply the parable of our art, we shall call the forest the *body*... The unicorn will be the *spirit* at all times. The deer desires no other name but that of the *soul*... He that knows how to tame and master them by art, to couple them together, and to lead them in and our of the form, may justly be called a Master."

The Egyptian devil, Typhon, was often symbolized by the *Set* monster whose identity is obscure. It has a queer snoutlike nose and pointed ears, and may have been a conventional hyena. The *Set* monster lived in the sand storms and wandered about the world promulgating evil. The Egyptians related the howling of the desert winds with the moaning cry of the hyena. Thus when in the depths of the night the hyena sent forth its doleful wail it sounded like the last despairing cry of a lost soul in the clutches of Typhon. Among the duties of this evil creature was that of protecting the Egyptian dead against grave robbers.

Among other symbols of Typhon was the hippopotamus, sacred to the god Mars because Mars was enthroned in the sign of Scorpio, the house of Typhon. The ass was also sacred to this Egyptian demon. Jesus riding into Jerusalem upon the back of an ass has the same significance as Hermes standing upon the prostrate form of Typhon. The early Christians were accused of worshiping the head of an ass. A most curious animal symbol is the hog or sow, sacred to Diana, and frequently employed in the Mysteries as an emblem of the occult art. The wild boar which gored Atys shows the use of this animal in the Mysteries.

According to the Mysteries, the monkey represents the condition of man before the rational soul entered into his constitution. Therefore it typifies the irrational man. By some the monkey is looked upon as a species not ensouled by the spiritual hierarchies; by others as a fallen state wherein man has been deprived of his divine nature through degeneracy. The ancients, though evolutionists, did not trace man's ascent through the monkey; the monkey they considered as having separated itself from the main stem of progress. The monkey was occasionally employed as a symbol of learning. Cynocephalus, the dog-headed ape, was the Egyptian hieroglyphic symbol of writing, and was closely associated with Thoth. Cynocephalus is symbolic of the moon and Thoth of the planet Mercury. Because of the ancient belief that the moon followed Mercury about the heavens the dog-ape was described as the faithful companion of Thoth.

The dog, because of its faithfulness, denotes the relationship which should exist between disciple and master or between the initiate and his God. The shepherd dog was a type of the priestcraft. The dog's ability to sense and follow unseen persons for miles symbolized the transcendental power by which the philosopher follows the thread of truth through the labyrinth of earthly error. The dog is also the symbol of Mercury. The Dog Star, Sirius or Sothis, was sacred to the Egyptians because it presaged the annual inundations of the Nile.

As a beast of burden the horse was the symbol of the body of man forced to sustain the weight of his spiritual constitution. Conversely, it also typified the spiritual nature of man forced to maintain the burden of the material personality. Chiron, the centaur, mentor of Achilles, represents the primitive creation which was the progenitor and instructor of mankind, as described by Berossus. The winged horse and the magic carpet both symbolize the secret doctrine and the spiritualized body of man. The wooden horse of Troy, secreting an army for the capture of the city, represents man's body concealing within it those infinite potentialities which will later come forth and conquer his environment. Again, like Noah's Ark, it represents the spiritual nature of man as containing a host of latent potentialities which subsequently become active. The siege of Troy is a symbolic account of the abduction of the human soul (Helena) by the personality (Paris) and its final redemption, through persevering struggle, by the secret doctrine--the Greek army under the command of Agamemnon.

www.ingramcontent.com/pod-product-compliance
Lightning Source LLC
LaVergne TN
LVHW041500070426
835507LV00009B/710